COLORING BOOK

25 TEACHER RELATED SAYINGS & EXPERIENCES

DEDICATION:

*This book is dedicated to all the teachers
that put in the time, work, and effort to
change children's lives daily.
You are the real influencers!*

BEST CLASS EVER: ALL THREE TROUBLEMAKERS ARE ABSENT TODAY!

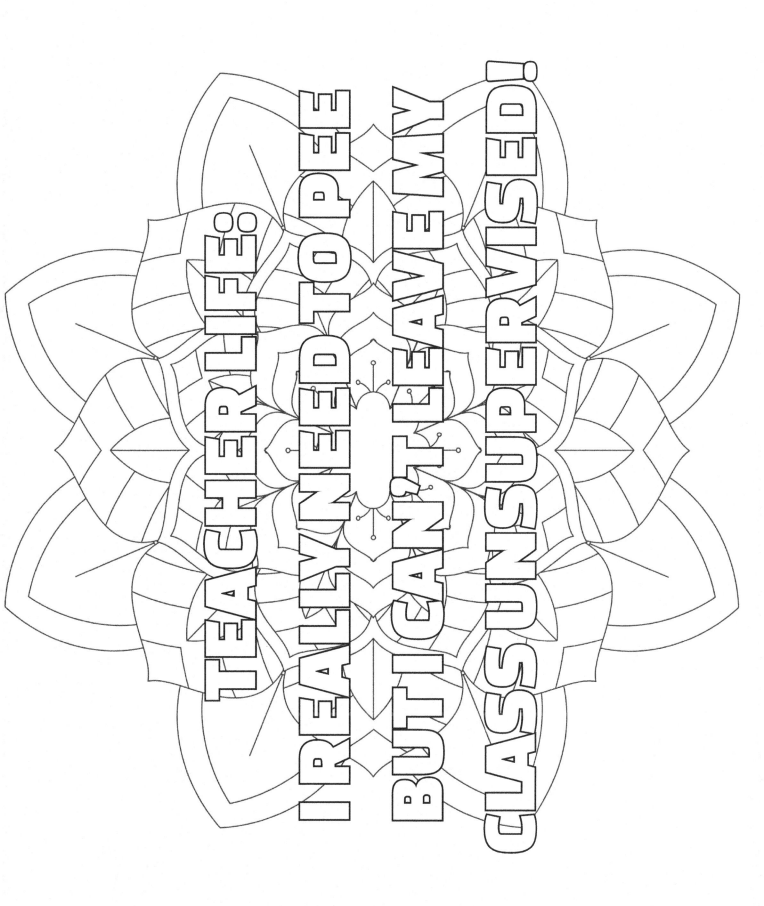

AVERAGE STARTING TEACHER SALARY: $34,000

AVERAGE CABLE TV INSTALLER SALARY $42,000

PRIORITIES, AMERICA!

WELCOME TO TEACHING, WHERE THE SALARIES ARE LOW AND EVERYTHING IS YOUR FAULT!

BEING A TEACHER IS EASY. IT'S LIKE RIDING A BIKE! RIDING A BIKE! BUT THE BIKE IS ON FIRE AND SO ARE YOU AND YOU AND YOU'RE IN A PIT OF FIRE!

TEACHER MICHMAR? TODAY I SAID "ORGASM INSTEAD OF ORGANISM...." IN FRONT OF THIRTY 13 YEAR OLDS!

TEACHING: THE ONLY PROFESSION WHERE YOU STEAL SUPPLIES FROM HOME AND BRING THEM TO WORK

COLORING BOOK

25 TEACHER RELATED SAYINGS & EXPERIENCES

DON'T FORGET TO LEAVE A
REVIEW ON AMAZON!

Made in the USA
Coppell, TX
04 January 2020